Bean and Chuff are having a treat. They are having a big fish pie to eat. Yum, yum.

Bean eats too much pie. He feels sick. He cries. He lies down on the grass. He soon goes to sleep.

Chuff eats the pie too fast. He gets a pain. He lies down on the grass. He soon goes to sleep.

Jelly comes to look for Bean. She sees him sleeping on the grass. She lies down next to him. She looks after him.

Jelly sees a magpie in a tree. She pretends to be asleep, but she spies on the magpie as it flies out of the tree.

The magpie flies down to the pie dish. It pecks at the fish in the dish. Oh no! ... The magpie gets a fish bone stuck in its beak.

The magpie tries to get rid of the fish bone. It bangs its beak on the pie dish. ... Oh no! ... The fish bone gets stuck in its throat.

Oh no! The fish bone will cut the magpie's throat. It will bleed. The magpie will die! Jelly must save it.

She bangs the magpie on its back. Bang ... bang! The fish bone falls in the pie dish.

The magpie thanks Jelly. Then it flies back to its tree. Jelly is a hero, and nobody knows. They are all asleep.

"ie"

pie

die

magpie

flies

cries

tries

spies

lies

High Frequency Words

the are a they big to she on it sees comes for look at no gets of is all he and look

too much down then him next be but tree will after back out as must